Magic, Myth, and Mystery

GENIES

DO YOU BELIEVE?

This series features creatures that excite our minds. They're magical. They're mythical. They're mysterious. They're also not real. They live in our stories. They're brought to life by our imaginations. Facts about these creatures are based on folklore, legends, and beliefs. We have a rich history of believing in the impossible. But these creatures only live in fantasies and dreams. Monsters do not live under our beds. They live in our heads!

45th Parallel Press

Published in the United States of America by Cherry Lake Publishing
Ann Arbor, Michigan
www.cherrylakepublishing.com

Reading Adviser: Marla Conn MS, Ed., Literacy specialist, Read-Ability, Inc.
Cover Design: Felicia Macheske

Photo Credits: © NemesisINC/Shutterstock.com, cover; © Olga Danylenko/Shutterstock.com, cover; © Audy39/Shutterstock.com, cover, 1; © Brian A Jackson/Shutterstock.com, 5; © welburnstuart/ Shutterstock.com, 7; © Iuliia Stepashova/Shutterstock.com, 8; © Suzanne Tucker/Shutterstock.com, 11; © Kateryna Upit/Shutterstock.com, 13; © Fotos593/Shutterstock.com, 14; © gwolters/Shutterstock.com, 17; © nikkytok/Shutterstock.com, 18; ©Praiwun Thungsarn/Shutterstock.com, 21; © Tokarchuk Andrii/ Shutterstock.com, 22; © Belovodchenko Anton/Shutterstock.com, 24; © Marcel Mooij/Shutterstock.com, 27; © Darla Hallmark/Shutterstock.com, 29

Graphic Elements Throughout: © denniro/Shutterstock.com; © Libellule/Shutterstock.com; © sociologas/ Shutterstock.com; © paprika/Shutterstock.com; © ilolab/Shutterstock.com; © Bruce Rolff/Shutterstock.com

45th Parallel Press is an imprint of Cherry Lake Publishing.

Library of Congress Cataloging-in-Publication Data has been filed and is available at catalog.loc.gov

Cherry Lake Publishing would like to acknowledge the work of The Partnership for 21st Century Skills.
Please visit *www.p21.org* for more information.

Printed in the United States of America
Corporate Graphics

TABLE of CONTENTS

Rubbing for Wishes

What are genies? Where do they live? What do they look like?

"Your wish is my command." Genies are magical beings. They live in **vessels**. Vessels are containers. Some live in bottles. Some live in **oil lamps**. Oil lamps hold oil. They use the oil to keep a flame burning.

Genies are **imprisoned** in vessels. They're trapped inside. They can be trapped for years. Then, people find the vessels. They rub the lamps or bottles. This rubbing releases the genies. It **summons** the genies. Summon means to call.

Genies **grant** three wishes to their **masters**. Grant means to give. Masters are people who summon genies. They're in charge of the genies.

Genies are sealed inside bottles or lamps.

Explained by Science!

Genies grant wishes. They're commanded to do so. There's a drug that makes people follow commands. This drug is called Devil's Breath. It's made from the flowers of a plant in the nightshade family. This plant is from South America. The seeds are turned into a powder. A chemical is taken out. It causes hallucinations. Hallucinations are when people think they see things that aren't there. The drug causes people to see scary things. It makes people feel like zombies. People can't control their actions. They do whatever others tell them. The drug also causes people to forget what happened. South American tribes gave it to the wives of dead chiefs. They buried wives alive with their husbands. This was a custom. The CIA also used the drug. They used it as truth medicine.

Genies live anywhere.

Genies give their masters three wishes. Then, they return to their vessels. They wait until they're found again.

Some people believe that a god made genies, humans, and angels. Genies are made from the "fire of a **scorching** wind." Scorching means really hot. Genies are made out of a fire that gives no smoke. Then, humans were made. They were made from earth. Angels are the souls of dead humans. They're made from light.

Genies formed their own cities. They made their own laws. But they made the god mad. The god broke up their cities. The god trapped them.

There are different types of genies. Most genies look like humans. But they're **supernatural**. Supernatural are things that can't be explained. They have special powers. They can live for thousands of years.

They come in all shapes and sizes. Some have thick fur on their legs. Some have **hooves**. Hooves are hard coverings over feet. Some genies have heads without bodies. Some have bodies without heads. Some are half-human. Some have human bodies. Some have fog for legs. Some genies have **tattoos**. These are colored ink designs on skin.

Genies can be male or female.

Chapter Two

Genius Powers of Genies

What are genies' powers? What are some rules about genies' wishes?

Genies are **mischievous**. This means they play jokes. Genies have **free will**. Free will is when people can make decisions by themselves. Genies can be good. They can be bad. They do what they want.

They make objects appear and disappear. They can change their shapes. They can become people. They can become animals. They can become fire.

They can become air. They can become water. They can be found everywhere. Their favorite shapes to take are snakes and black dogs. Some genies can make themselves **invisible**. Invisible means they can't be seen.

Some genies kidnap women and children.

When Fantasy Meets Reality!

The bluebottle jellyfish looks like a genie in a bottle. It's not one animal. It's a group of four zooids. The zooids are like animals. They work together. They form what looks like a jellyfish. The animals depend on each other. That's how they live. The float is the main zooid. It supports the rest of the animals. It's blue. It looks like a sail. The tentacles are the arms. They capture food. They sting. Another zooid acts like a stomach. It eats the prey. Another zooid has babies. It has both female and male parts. Bluebottles live in Australia. They use winds to travel. Winds push across the surface of the water. Winds blow them onto the beach. Humans who touch them wish that they hadn't. Bluebottles give sharp, painful stings.

Some genies control weather.

Some genies can read people's minds. They learn people's deepest wishes. These genies don't really grant wishes. They poison people by touching them. Their touch makes people see things. They send people into a fantasy world. They make some people live in their dreams. They make some people live in their nightmares. This is how genies trick people. They do this to feed on human blood.

Some genies can fly. Ampharool is one of the world's oldest genies. He teaches men how to fly.

Genies **manipulate** wishes. Manipulate means to twist words. It means to distort wishes. Genies can change people's wishes. Bad or strange things could happen. Getting wishes isn't always a good thing.

Genies have rules for wishes. They limit masters' powers. Masters can't wish to be a god. They can't wish for death. They can't wish for more wishes. But masters can wish for genies to be their slaves. They have to take care of their masters. They can only do regular things. Genies can cook. They can clean. But they can't affect the universe. Masters can't let other people touch the vessel. If this happens, the new person becomes the new master.

Genies can choose to help or hurt masters.

Chapter Three

Stop the Genies!

What are genies' weaknesses? What are signs of genies being nearby? What are some ways to kill genies?

Genies have weaknesses. They can't travel far from their vessels. They can't talk to the dead. They can't bring people to life.

They can't mess with free will. They can't force people to fall in love. They can't kill. But they can give weapons or powers. They can attack. They can cause pain.

Genies can be invisible. But animals can see them. Some people think donkeys' **brays** means genies are nearby. Brays are donkey noises. Some people think genies are nearby when cats stare. Some people think children can see genies.

Some people think crowing roosters means angels are nearby.

Genie lamps and bottles are magical prisons.

There are other signs that genies are nearby. The air changes. It can become cooler. It can become warmer. Pets run away in fear.

Some genies get stuck in their lamps or bottles. They get stuck for a long time. Their power builds up. Their energy bursts out. The genies kill themselves.

There are other ways to kill genies. A silver knife dipped in lamb's blood can kill genies. Reading holy verses can kill genies. Destroying the vessel can kill genies. But vessels are hard to destroy.

SURVIVAL TIPS!

- Don't force genies out of your lives. If they don't want to leave, they won't. Use one of your wishes to get them to go.

- Lock your doors. Genies steal things. But they won't open locked doors.

- Tie knots. Genies can't untie knots.

- Don't use candlelight. Genies take away wicks. They start fires.

- Don't harm or try to kill genies. They'll get revenge.

- Don't upset genies. They remember everything.

- Don't wish for a genie's freedom. You'll take its place. You'll become a genie.

Chapter Four

Hidden History

How were the vessels hidden? Where do genies come from? What are the different types of genies?

Vessels are made of gold, silver, and magic. Angels added the magic. They tried to control genies. They wanted to distract genies. They created a fantasy world inside the vessel. This kept genies from escaping. This kept them busy. They waited for masters.

Angels put the vessels in a special **temple**. The temple is underground. Temples are like churches. Angels allowed people to make wishes. But people went crazy. They became selfish. They stole the vessels. Angels came. They took the vessels back. They scattered them around the world. They hid them.

Genies need to be released every once in a while.

Stories about genies are from the Middle East. They're in *The Arabian Nights*. This is a collection of stories. Genies are also in the **Koran**. The Koran is the holy book of Muslims. Genies were called **jinn**. Jinn is an Arabic word. It means "to hide."

Antoine Galland was a French man. He had a copy of *The Arabian Nights*. He was the first European to translate the book. He did this in 1704. He changed *jinn* to *genie*. The word genie comes from a Latin word. The Latin word is genius. Genius is a guardian spirit of people and places.

Genies are most popular in stories from the Middle East.

Know the Lingo!

- **Azazel:** prince of darkness

- **Djinn:** very powerful genies

- **Iblis:** highest ranked genie

- **Jinni:** one genie

- **Jinnistan:** name of a place genies live

- **Kaf:** magical emerald mountains surrounding the earth where genies live

- **Marid:** strongest type of genie that lives in a vessel and grants wishes

- **Shaytan:** Satan, the master djinn

- **Wind jinn:** a type of winged genie that can fly quickly

There are many types of genies. Different parts of the Middle East believe in them.

The ghul change shapes. They drink blood. They eat human meat. They eat travelers. They eat children. They eat dead bodies from graves. They hunt at night. Ghulas are female. They look like human women. They marry human men. Then, they eat them.

The jann are the weakest genies. They change shapes. They live in the desert. They fight ghuls.

The palis live in the desert. They're not smart. They can be tricked. They attack sleeping people. They drain their blood. They do this by licking their feet.

Flying genies may have inspired vampire stories.

Chapter Five

Aladdin's Magic Lamp

Who is Aladdin? What is his story?

Stories about genies come from *The Arabian Nights*. Aladdin's lamp is the most popular.

Aladdin is a poor young man. He meets a **sorcerer**. Sorcerers are like wizards. The sorcerer pretends to be Aladdin's uncle. He turns Aladdin into a rich salesman. He tricks Aladdin. He wants Aladdin to get an oil lamp. The oil lamp is in a cave. The cave has many hidden traps. The sorcerer gives Aladdin a magic ring. He says the ring is protection.

Aladdin gets stuck in the cave. He rubs his head. He ends up rubbing the ring. A genie appears. The genie frees Aladdin. Aladdin goes home. He has the oil lamp.

The Arabian Nights *has been around for hundreds of years.*

Real-World Connection

The Make-A-Wish Foundation is a special organization. It helps children who have serious sicknesses. The children must be between ages 3 and 17. The organization grants them wishes. John Cena has granted the most wishes. He's granted over 500 wishes. He's a professional wrestling superstar. He's also an actor. He gives children good seats to his wrestling events. He gives them gifts. He gives them a party. He visits hospitals. He started granting wishes in 2004. He also donates money and airline miles. He said, "I want them to have an experience that will stay with them forever. I don't ever want the children or their families to be treated in a way where they feel as if they're up against anything at all."

This story popularized genies coming out of lamps.

Aladdin's mother cleans the lamp. A more powerful genie appears. He gives Aladdin wishes. Aladdin becomes rich. He marries a princess.

The sorcerer hears of Aladdin's riches. He tricks the princess. He trades new lamps for old lamps. He takes control of the genie. He takes Aladdin's riches.

But Aladdin still has the magic ring. He summons the other genie. The genie helps Aladdin. Aladdin gets the lamp back. He kills the sorcerer. He gets his riches back.

The sorcerer's brother gets mad. He dresses as an old woman to trick Aladdin. But Aladdin's genie told him of the trick. Aladdin kills the brother. He becomes king.

Did You Know?

- *The Arabian Nights* is also called *One Thousand and One Nights*.

- The Mende people live in Sierra Leone. This is in Africa. The Mende believe in genies. Their genies enter the bodies of living men.

- Ancient Romans believed in genies. Their genies watched over men. These genies formed men's characters. They caused men's actions. They were present at birth. Evil genies fought good genies for control of a man's fate.

- Flying genies eavesdrop on the angels. They tell fortune-tellers what they hear. But they lie. They add extra details.

- Some people think genies have special colors. Blue genies are older and smart. Yellow genies are leaders. Green genies are young and playful. Black genies are powerful. Red genies are dangerous.

- Some stories say there are genies living in the Bermuda Triangle. Some genies live on the seafloor. These genies live in their bottles or lamps for a very long time.

- Genies change when they use their powers. Their eyes and hands glow blue. Their tattoos move on their skin.

- Some genies like living in dirty places. They live in graveyards, garbage dumps, bathrooms, and animal poop.

- Some people think every human is born with a genie. Genies watch over people. They mess with people. They see if people can tell right from wrong. They test people's free will.

Consider This!

Take a Position: Some people think genies are good. Some people think genies are evil. What do you think? Are genies good or evil? Argue your point with reasons and evidence.

Say What? Genies grant wishes. What would you wish for? Explain your wishes. Explain your reasons.

Think About It! There's a quote about genies. It is: "You can't get the genie back in the bottle." What do you think the quote means? What are other quotes about genies?

Learn More

- Marsico, Katie. *Magic Monsters: From Witches to Goblins*. Minneapolis: Lerner Publications, 2017.

- Napoli, Donna Jo, and Christina Balit (illustrator). *Tales from the Arabian Nights: Stories of Adventure, Magic, Love, and Betrayal*. Washington, DC: National Geographic Partners, 2016.

Glossary

brays (BRAYZ) donkey sounds

free will (FREE WIL) having the ability to make one's own decisions and decide between right and wrong

grant (GRANT) to give

hooves (HOOVZ) hard coverings over feet

imprisoned (im-PRIZ-uhnd) jailed, trapped

invisible (in-VIZ-ih-buhl) not being seen

jinn (GIN) Arabic word for genies meaning "to hide"

Koran (kuh-RAN) holy book of Muslims

manipulate (muh-NIP-yoo-late) to twist or distort

masters (MAS-turz) owners, people in charge of something

mischievous (MIS-chuh-vuhs) naughty, playing jokes

oil lamps (OIL LAMPS) containers that use oil to make light

scorching (SKORCH-ing) really hot

sorcerer (SOR-sur-er) wizard or magician

summons (SUHM-uhnz) calls

supernatural (soo-pur-NACH-ur-uhl) things that can't be explained

tattoos (tah-TOOZ) colored ink designs on skin

temple (TEM-puhl) churchlike building

vessels (VES-uhlz) containers

Index

About the Author

Dr. Virginia Loh-Hagan is an author, university professor, former classroom teacher, and curriculum designer. Her husband is her genie. He does whatever she wishes. She lives in San Diego with her very tall husband and very naughty dogs. To learn more about her, visit www.virginialoh.com.